PALEO SLOW COOKER

SOUPS & STEWS FOR PEOPLE WHO LOVE TO EAT

GLUTEN, GRAIN & DAIRY FREE SOUPS THAT WILL WARM YOUR HEART & YOUR STOMACH

Elizabeth Vine

ISBN: 1508572836
ISBN-13: 978-1508572831

DEDICATION

There's just something that warms the heart when you can snuggle up with a bowl of steaming hot soup or stew on a cold winter's day.

Maybe it's reminiscent of sick days as a kid when that was the only thing that would make you feel better.
Maybe its dinner at grandma's house and her delicious chicken noodle made just the way she knew you'd like it.
Maybe it's the way a cup of soup warms every inch of your body on a freezing cold day when nothing else can.

It's comfort in a cup.

We've put 17 delicious soup and stew recipes together in this guide for you that include favorites like Chicken Noodle and Minestrone, to international flavors like Mexican Meatball and Thai Butternut Squash all the way to Irish Guinness Stew. Can you say yummy?

Each of the 17 recipes have detailed step by step simple instructions, cooking times, prep times and number of servings and are all 100% Gluten-free, 100% Dairy-free and 100% Sugar-free.

With so many health benefits and nutritional value soups are a great way to get your daily vegetable servings and fill up quickly. We suggest doubling the recipes and making them in batches on a Sunday or free evening. Then simply keep in the fridge for 3-5 days and you've got soup for the rest of the week!

Loves,

Elizabeth Vine

Paleo Wired
Gather.Eat.Repeat

.Important Legal Disclaimer:

CONTENTS

1 **SOUPS**

MUSHROOM BACON SOUP

SERVES: 4-6
PREP TIME: 7 min
COOK TIME: 25 min

Ingredients:

2 lbs brown mushrooms
1 lb white mushrooms
2" chunk of back bacon
1 small onion
2 garlic cloves
½ whole celery root
1 Tbsp Avocado Oil (or melted coconut oil)
2 tsp pepper
Sea Salt to taste

Directions:

1.   Using a damp paper towel, wipe the mushrooms clean and chop into quarters.
2.   Cut the back bacon into small pieces and chop all the vegetables into equally sized pieces.
3.   In a deep saucepan, heat oil over medium temperature and add bacon.
4.   Cook for 2-3 minutes, and then add all ingredients and fry for 5-7 minutes until mushrooms are brown and cooked.
5.   Add 5 cups of water and bring everything to a boil, adding salt and pepper.
6.   Simmer for 10-15 minutes until vegetables are thoroughly cooked.
7.   Run entire mixture through a blender until completely smooth.
8.   Put back onto stove and cook for another 2-3 minutes.
9.   Garnish with chopped fresh parsley.
10.   Serve & Enjoy!

GRANDMA'S EASY CHICKEN NOODLE

SERVES: 4-6
PREP TIME: 5 min
COOK TIME: 1h 25min

Ingredients:

2 lbs chicken (thighs, bones, neck)
3 carrots
4 celery sticks
1 medium onion
4-5 parsley leaves
2 eggs
2 tsp Sea Salt
1 tsp Ground Pepper
2 tsp Herb Mix (dried Oregano, Parsley, Basil, and Thyme)

Directions:

1. Fill a large, deep cooking pot ¾ full of water.
2. Wash and cut the carrots, celery and onion into threes and add to the pot.
3. Add the chicken pieces into the pot.
4. Add the parsley into the pot.
5. Put on medium-high temperature and bring to boil.
6. Simmer for 1 hour and 15 minutes until chicken is cooked all the way through.
7. Remove chicken thighs and strain remaining soup into another pot.
8. Use a fork to remove the skin of chicken thighs and shred the meat off the bone into small pieces.
9. Cut the carrots into bite sized pieces and put back into the pot, along with the shredded chicken.
10. Add the spices and bring to a boil.
11. Crack 2 eggs directly into the mixture for faux noodles and cook for 1-2 minutes.
12. Serve & Enjoy!

THAI BUTTERNUT SQUASH SOUP

SERVES: 4 - 6
PREP TIME: 5 min
COOK TIME: 25 min

Ingredients:

1 large butternut squash
1 -12oz can full fat coconut milk
3 cups low-sodium vegetable stock (or homemade soup stock)
3 garlic cloves
1" piece of fresh ginger, minced
½ onion
2 Tbsp coconut oil
2 Tbsp red curry paste
2 Tbsp lime juice
1 Tbsp freshly chopped cilantro
1 tsp Sea salt
½ tsp Pepper

Directions:

1.   Wash and peel the butternut squash with a potato peeler.
2.   Cut into 1" chunks and set aside.
3.   Chop ½ onion and mince the garlic cloves.
4.   Heat 2 Tbsp coconut oil over medium heat and add the onion, cooking until translucent (3-5 minutes).
5.   Add the minced garlic cloves and cook another 1 minute (before it starts to brown!).
6.   Add the curry paste and ginger and cook for 5 minutes.
7.   Now add in the soup stock and butternut squash chunks and simmer for 15-20 minutes until squash is soft.
8.   Run the entire mixture through a blender until completely smooth.
9.   Pour the pureed soup back into the pot and add the coconut milk, lime, salt and pepper stirring well.
10.   Cook for another 10 -12 minutes covered.
11.   Top with freshly chopped cilantro.
12.   Serve & Enjoy!

MEXICAN MEATBALL SOUP

SERVES: 4 - 6
PREP TIME: 5 min
COOK TIME: 25 min

Ingredients:

For the Meatballs:

½ lb grass-fed ground beef
1 jalapeno pepper
2 garlic cloves
1 tsp chili powder
½ tsp turmeric
1 tsp dried oregano
½ tsp sea salt
½ tsp pepper
1 Tbsp arrowroot powder
1 egg

For the Soup:

4 cups all natural organic chicken or vegetable broth (or homemade soup stock)
1 – 12oz can crushed tomatoes
2 cups water
2 small zucchinis
1 red onion
1 small lime, juiced
1-2 fresh parsley leaves
1 Teaspoon Chili Flakes
1 Teaspoon Cayenne Pepper
1 tsp dried oregano
1 Tbsp Avocado Oil (or melted coconut oil)
Sea Salt
Pepper

Directions:

For the Meatballs:

1. Mince the garlic cloves and ½ the jalapeno pepper (removing the seeds).
2. Add into a medium bowl along with ground beef and spices.
3. Add arrowroot powder and egg and mix altogether well.
4. Make 1'x1' meatballs (mixture should make 20-25 bite sized meatballs).

For the Soup:

5. Dice the red onion and cut the zucchini into bite sized pieces.
6. In a large saucepan, heat the avocado oil over medium temperature.
7. Add the onion and remaining ½ jalapeno pepper and sauté for 3-5 minutes until onion starts to become translucent.
8. Add the zucchini and spices and cook for 3-4 minutes, until zucchini becomes soft.
9. Add the water, broth and can of crushed tomatoes and simmer for 13-15 minutes.
10. Add the meatballs to the soup, and simmer until they're cooked (5-7 minutes).
11. Turn the heat off, add 1 Tbsp lime juice and mix well.
12. Serve & Enjoy!

PALEO MINESTRONE

SERVES: 4 - 6
PREP TIME: 5 min
COOK TIME: 20 min

Ingredients:

2 cups zoodles (zucchini noodles)
½ cup chorizo sausage
1 medium onion
2 carrots
4 celery sticks
2 garlic cloves
1 – 18 oz can diced tomatoes
1 cup water
1 bundle fresh spinach
1 Tbsp fresh basil
2 Tbsp Avocado Oil (or melted coconut oil)
1 tsp chili flakes
½ tsp Sea salt
½ tsp Pepper

Directions:

1.   Using a mandolin/spiralizer or very sharp knife, cut 3-4 zucchinis into equally sized spaghetti-like noodles (zoodles). Set aside.
2.   Cut the onion and mince the garlic cloves.
3.   Wash and chop the carrots and celery sticks into small ½" thick circular pieces.
4.   Heat 2 Tbsp avocado oil in a large saucepan over medium heat.
5.   Add the onion and cook 3-4 minutes until translucent.
6.   Add minced garlic cloves, chorizo sausage, carrots and celery sticks and cook another 3-4 minutes.
7.   Stir in the can of diced tomatoes, water and spices and simmer for 10 minutes.
8.   Add the zoodles and cook for another 3-5 minutes, until zucchini is tender.
9.   Stir in the spinach and top with freshly chopped basil.
10.   Serve & Enjoy!

VIETNAMESE PORK PHO

SERVES: 4
PREP TIME: 20 min
COOK TIME: 30 min

Ingredients:

2 – 12oz pork shoulder steaks
7 - 8 cups low-sodium chicken broth
1 medium onion
2 garlic cloves
1 lime
1 cinnamon stick
2 star anise
1 tsp fennel seeds
1" piece fresh ginger
½ tsp chili flakes
2 Tbsp Avocado Oil (or melted coconut oil)
1/3 cup fresh Alfalfa sprouts
Fresh Cilantro leaves

Directions:

1.   Peel the onion and cut into half.
2.   In a skillet over medium-high temp, cook the onion halves, cut side down, until charred (4-5 minutes). Set aside.
3.   Add the chili flakes, fennel seeds, minced garlic, cinnamon stick and star anise pods and cook for 1 minute, until start to smell the fragrance.
4.   Transfer to a saucepan and add the charred onion, minced ginger root and broth, bringing to a boil over med-high temperature.
5.   Simmer for 10-15 minutes, until broth is full of flavor.
6.   Season pork shoulder with salt and pepper.
7.   Heat 2 Tbsp oil on the skillet, and when hot, sear the pork on all sides (about 3 minutes on each side). Set aside for 5 minutes then slice into thin pieces.
8.   Ladle soup mixture into bowls; add sliced pork pieces and fresh alfalfa sprouts and cilantro leaves.
9.   Serve & Enjoy!

CAULIFLOWER LEEK SOUP

SERVES: 4 - 6
PREP TIME: 5 min
COOK TIME: 25 min

Ingredients:

1 cup chicken or vegetable stock
1 cup water
1 head of cauliflower
1 leek
1 medium onion
2 garlic cloves
1 celery stick
2 Tbsp Avocado Oil (or melted coconut oil)
1 tsp Turmeric
1 tsp Chili flakes
½ tsp Sea salt
½ tsp Pepper

Directions:

1. Wash and cut the cauliflower florets into evenly sized pieces.
2. Chop the leek, half the onion and celery stick. Mince the garlic cloves.
3. Heat 2 Tbsp oil in a saucepan over medium heat.
4. Add the onions and cook 3-4 minutes until translucent.
5. Add the garlic, celery and leek and cook another 2-3 minutes.
6. Add the cauliflower florets and spices and cook for 5-7 minutes, until everything is easily pierced with a fork.
7. Add the stock and water and bring to a boil, simmering for 10-12 minutes.
8. Puree entire soup in a blender and transfer back to the pot.
9. Cook for another 3-4 minutes, adding more salt and pepper to taste.
10. Serve & Enjoy!

ROASTED CARROT SOUP

SERVES: 4 - 6
PREP TIME: 7 min
COOK TIME: 25 min

Ingredients:

10 – 12 medium carrots
2-3 parsnips
2 celery sticks
1 small onion
2 Tbsp Avocado Oil
2 cups chicken or vegetable stock
1 tsp Sea Salt
1 tsp Pepper
1 tsp freshly grated ginger

Directions:

1.   Wash and peel the carrots and parsnips.
2.   Cut the carrots, parsnips and celery sticks into equal sized chunks.
Chop ½ the onion.
3.   Heat 2 Tbsp Avocado Oil in a medium saucepan.
4.   Add the onions and cook until translucent.
5.   Add the carrots, parsnips and celery sticks and sauté for 5-7 minutes,
until tender.
6.   Add the stock and spices and bring to a boil.
7.   Simmer 7-10 minutes, then puree in a blender until smooth.
8.   Top with freshly grated ginger.
9.   Serve & Enjoy!

YAM & SWISS CHARD CREAMY SOUP

SERVES: 4 - 6
PREP TIME: 5 min
COOK TIME: 30 min

Ingredients:

4 cups chicken or vegetable broth
1 cup water
3 medium yams
1 bundle fresh Swiss chard
1 medium onion
3 garlic cloves
1' piece fresh ginger
2 Tbsp Avocado Oil (or melted coconut oil)
1 tsp Chili Flakes
1 tsp Cayenne Pepper
1 tsp Sea Salt

Directions:

1. Wash and peel the yams, cutting into evenly shaped squares
2. Chop the onion and mince the garlic and ginger.
3. In a large saucepan, heat 2 Tbsp oil over medium temperature.
4. Add the onions and cook for 2-3 minutes, then add garlic cloves and ginger.
5. Wash and rip apart the Swiss chard leaves right into the saucepan, sautéing with the onion mixture for 5-6 minutes.
6. Add the yams, stock, water and spices and bring to a boil.
7. Simmer for 25 – 30 minutes, until yams are easily pierced through with a fork.
8. Puree entire mixture in a blender until smooth.
9. Cook another 5 minutes in the pan, stirring continuously.
10. Serve & Enjoy!

BACON CREAM OF GREENS SOUP

SERVES: 4 - 6
PREP TIME: 5 min
COOK TIME: 20 min

Ingredients:

3 slices of bacon
1 bundle of kale
1 green pepper
1 head of broccoli
1 medium onion
2 cups unsweetened almond milk
1 Tbsp onion powder
1 tsp Sea salt
½ tsp Pepper
1/3 cup crushed walnuts
1 tsp coconut oil, melted

Directions:

1.   Preheat the oven to 350F.
2.   Line a baking sheet with some parchment paper.
3.   Add the crushed walnuts and drizzle with a teaspoon of melted coconut oil.
4.   Put in the oven for 4-7 minutes, until start to get crunchy. Set aside.
5.   In a medium saucepan, put bacon slices directly into pan over medium temperature.
6.   Cook until crispy on each side, about 4-5 minutes.
7.   Remove bacon from pan, leaving grease aside. Crush with a paper towel into small pieces.
8.   Add ½ chopped onion into the bacon grease and cook 2-3 minutes. Add in diced green pepper and kale and sauté for 5-7 minutes until start to become tender.
9.   Add in half the broccoli florets, bacon bits, almond milk and salt and pepper to taste and simmer for 10 – 12 minutes.
10. Puree the entire mixture in a blender until smooth and add back to saucepan.
11.   Add in remaining broccoli florets and onion powder and cook another 10 minutes.
12. Top with crunchy walnuts from the oven.
13. Serve & Enjoy!

2 STEWS

IRISH GUINESS LAMB STEW

SERVES: 4 - 6
PREP TIME: 10 min
COOK TIME: 2hr

Ingredients:

3 lbs lamb shoulder
3 carrots
5 celery stalks
2 medium onions
4 garlic cloves
8 cups low-sodium beef broth
1 can of Guinness
3 Tbsp Avocado Oil
1 bundle fresh Rosemary
1 bundle Fresh Thyme
1 bundle Fresh Parsley
1 Tbsp Arrowroot Powder
1 Tsp Sea salt
½ tsp Pepper

Directions:

1.   Wash and cut the carrots and celery stalks into evenly sized bite-sized pieces.
2.   Chop the onion and mince the garlic.
3.   In a large saucepan, heat 3 Tbsp avocado oil over medium temperature.
4.   Add the salt and pepper onto the lamb, and sear the lamb shoulder for 3-4 minutes on each side, until completely brown. Set aside.
5.   Add the onions, carrots, celery and garlic to the pan and sauté for 4-5 minutes.
6.   Add the can of Guinness, and cook for 4-5 minutes mixing well with the vegetables and fat juices.
7.   Put the lamb shoulder back in the saucepan, and add the beef broth. Add water to make sure everything is covered, if needed.
8.   Add the spices and bring to a boil.
9.   Simmer for 2 hours, or until the lamb is tender.
10.   Add arrowroot powder to thicken, and salt and pepper to taste. Cook for another 2-3 minutes.
11.   Top with freshly chopped parsley.
12.   Serve & Enjoy!

SPICY PUMPKIN CHORIZO STEW

SERVES: 4 - 6
PREP TIME: 5 min
COOK TIME: 20 min

Ingredients:

1 medium pumpkin
1 cup thickly sliced chorizo sausage
1 medium onion
1 Bundle Fresh Parsley
1 – 24 oz tomato puree
2 tsp cayenne pepper
Sea Salt
Pepper

Directions:

1.   Clean out the pumpkin by removing the seeds and insides. Cut into evenly (bite) sized square chunks and peel.
2.   In a large saucepan over medium heat, cook the chorizo sausage for 1-2 minutes until it starts to release its oil. Set aside.
3.   Add the chopped onion into the pan and cook 5 minutes until translucent.
4.   Add the sausage back in, along with the spices, pumpkin and can of tomato puree.
5.   Simmer for 20 minutes, until pumpkin is cooked all the way through. Add salt and pepper to taste. If necessary, add a little water for desired texture – remember this is a stew so it should be chunky not full of liquid.
6.   Top with freshly chopped parsley.
7.   Serve & Enjoy!

BEEF & BROCCOLI STEW

SERVES: 4 - 6
PREP TIME: 10 min
COOK TIME: 30 min

Ingredients:

1 lb stir-fry beef sirloin
1 medium onion
4 cups beef broth
1 head of broccoli
1 tsp garlic powder
1 tsp oregano
2 Tbsp Avocado Oil
Sea Salt
Pepper

Directions:

1.   In a bowl, add 1 tsp Avocado oil, garlic powder, salt and pepper and coat the beef sirloin pieces.
2.   Heat 2 Tbsp Avocado Oil in a saucepan over medium heat.
3.   Add the beef and cook for 5-6 minutes, until starts to turn brown.
4.   Add the chopped onion and cook another 5 minutes.
5.   Add the broth and spices and bring to a boil.
6.   Simmer for 10 -12 minutes, and then add the broccoli. Continue to simmer another 5 minutes until broccoli starts to become tender.
7.   Serve & Enjoy!

TURKEY CHILI

SERVES: 4 -6
PREP TIME: 5 min
COOK TIME: 25 min

Ingredients:

½ lb (250g) ground turkey meat
1 can nitrate-free Organic tomato sauce
1 zucchini
1 cauliflower
1 carrot
1 tomato
1 medium onion
3 garlic cloves
1 bay leaf
1 tsp Chili flakes
1 tsp Paprika
2 Tbsp Avocado Oil (or melted coconut oil)
1 Tbsp freshly chopped parsley (or cilantro)
Sea salt
Pepper
½ cup Organic sulphite-free Red Wine (*optional)
½ cup Organic sulphite-free White Wine (*optional)

Directions:

1. Dice ½ the onion and garlic cloves into small pieces and set aside.
2. Wash and cut the cauliflower, zucchini, tomato and carrot into small bite-sized pieces.
3. In a saucepan over medium temperature, heat 2 tbsp of frying oil.
4. Add the onion and cook 1-2 minutes until translucent.
5. Add chopped garlic and cook for 1 minute.
6. Add the ground turkey meat and cook until all meat turns grey/brown, no more red meat remains.
7. Add the carrot and cauliflower pieces and cook for 2-3 minutes covered.
8. Add zucchini and tomato and cook for another 2 minutes.

9. Now add the can of tomato paste, ½ cup of water, spices and wine (if using).
10. Cover and let cook for 5-7 minutes.
11. Stir and let simmer uncovered for 10-15 minutes.
12. Add more spices to taste preference.
13. Top with fresh chopped parsley or cilantro on top.
14. Serve & Enjoy!

MEDITERRANEAN BRODETTO (FISH STEW)

SERVES: 4
PREP TIME: 5 min
COOK TIME: 20 min

Ingredients:

2 lbs (~1 kg) of variety of fish (tuna, salmon, cod, spelt mixture)
2 medium onions
5 garlic cloves
1 -12 oz can nitrite-free Organic tomato sauce
½ cup white wine (*optional)
2 Tbsp Fresh parsley
2 Tbsp Avocado Oil (or melted coconut oil)
Sea Salt
Pepper

Directions:

1. Clean and dice the onions.
2. Clean the fish and cut into evenly sized pieces for cooking.
3. In a medium saucepan, heat frying oil of choice over medium temperature.
4. Add the onion and cook for 3-4 minutes.
5. Add the tomato sauce and ½ cup of white wine or water.
6. Bring to a boil and add fish, garlic, and Sea Salt and pepper.
7. Cook for 10-15 minutes until fish is cooked well.
8. Top with freshly chopped parsley.
9. Serve & Enjoy!

CHICKEN VERDE & SAUSAGE STEW

SERVES: 4 - 6
PREP TIME: 20 min
COOK TIME: 1h 45min

Ingredients:

1 whole chicken
3-4 spicy sausages (chorizo or personal preference)
4-5 pieces of kale
8-10 tomatillos
2 jalapeno pepper
5 garlic cloves
3 ½ cups all natural chicken stock (or homemade)
1 medium onion
4 Tbsp Avocado Oil
2 tsp ground cumin
2 tsp dried Oregano
1 bay leaf
Bundle Fresh Cilantro
Sea Salt
Pepper

Directions:

1.   Cut the jalapeno peppers in half, and the tomatillos in quarters.
2.   Line onto a baking sheet, and drizzle with Avocado Oil.
3.   Put on broil for 4-5 minutes, until start to brown. Set aside.
4.   Heat 2 Tbsp Avocado Oil in a saucepan over medium heat.
5.   Cut the chicken with a sharp knife or scissors into 5-6 equally sized pieces.
6.   Coat with 1 tsp sea salt and 1 tsp pepper.

7.   Sear chicken pieces in the pan 5-7 minutes each until brown on all sides. Set aside.

8.   Place roasted tomatillos and jalapeno peppers, along with minced garlic cloves, half of the cilantro bundle chopped well and the soup stock in a blender and puree.

9.   In the saucepan, heat another 2 Tbsp Avocado Oil and add chopped onion.

10.   Cook until onion is translucent, about 5-7 minutes.

11.   Cut up the sausages into bite sized pieces and add to the pan.

12.   Add in the cumin, oregano and bay leaf and cook another 3-4 minutes.

13.   Add the chicken pieces and pureed mixture and bring to a boil.

14.   Simmer for 1 hour and 10 minutes, until chicken is cooked through and easily falls off the bone.

15.   Break up the kale leaves into bite sized pieces and add into the mixture at the 45 minute mark.

16.   Remove the chicken pieces and using a fork carefully separate all the meat off the bones. Add back into simmering mixture.

17.   Add more salt and pepper to taste and cook for 1-2 minutes with chicken, stirring.

18.   Serve & Enjoy!

SWEET POTATO COCONUT CURRY

SERVES: 4 - 6
PREP TIME: 5 min
COOK TIME: 55 min

Ingredients:

3 large sweet potatoes
1 – 12 oz can coconut milk
1 – 8oz can tomatoes
1 small onion
2 garlic cloves
1" piece fresh ginger
1 Tbsp freshly parsley, chopped
1 Tbsp Avocado Oil
2 Tbsp coconut oil
1 fresh chili pepper
½ tsp dried cumin
½ tsp dried turmeric
½ tsp coriander
½ tsp ground cloves
1 Teaspoon Sea Salt
½ tsp pepper

Directions:

1.   Preheat the oven to 400F.
2.   Cut the sweet potatoes into chunks and coat with Avocado Oil (about 1 Tbsp), ½ tsp salt and pepper.
3.   Place evenly on a baking sheet and bake for 20-25 minutes, until sweet potato is easily pierced with a fork.
4.   Remove and peel the sweet potato chunks.
5.   Combine all spices into a small bowl.

6.   Over medium heat, melt 2 Tbsp coconut oil.

7.   Cook chopped onion 3-5 minutes until translucent.

8.   Add minced garlic cloves, chili pepper, minced fresh ginger and ½ the spice mixture and cook with the onions for another 2-3 minutes.

9.   Add in the coconut milk, canned tomatoes, roasted sweet potato chunks and remaining spice mixture.

10.   Simmer for 10-15 minutes, mixing well.

11.   Puree entire soup in a blender until completely smooth.

12.   Top with freshly chopped parsley.

13.   Serve & Enjoy!

A NOTE OF THANKS

Thank you for purchasing
PALEO SLOW COOKER - SOUPS & STEWS FOR PEOPLE WHO
LOVE TO EAT.

We hope you enjoyed making and eating the recipes as much as we enjoyed
putting them together (and testing them!!).

Now that you've seen how delicious eating Paleo is and you're ready to
make it a Lifestyle – we've put together a **FREE THANK YOU GIFT** for
you.

If we can take a second and ask you for a small favor??
If you enjoyed this book please let us an honest review on Amazon.com.
Reviews are so important for independent authors like us and it would
mean a huge amount if you took the 2 minutes to write one.
I do look forward to reading your review, thank you kindly in advance!

Head to WWW.PALEOWIRED.COM for your FREE GUIDE:

10 QUICK & EASY STEPS TO GO PALEO

Made in the USA
Middletown, DE
24 December 2016